Top Dogs

Columbus, OH • Chicago, IL • Redmond, WA

The **McGraw·Hill** *Companies*

The Independent Reading Books

The ***Independent Reading Books*** are reading books that fill the need for easy-to-read stories for the primary grades. The appeal of these stories will encourage independent reading at the early grade levels.

The stories focus on the Dolch 220 Basic Sight Vocabulary and the 95 Common Nouns. Beyond these lists, the books use about three new words per page.

This series was prepared under the direction and supervision of Edward W. Dolch, Ph.D.

This revision was prepared under the direction and supervision of Eleanor Dolch LaRoy and the Dolch Family Trust.

SRAonline.com

 **SRA**

Send all inquiries to:
SRA/McGraw-Hill
8787 Orion Place
Columbus, OH 43240-4027

Printed in the United States of America.

ISBN 0-07-602526-8

2 3 4 5 6 7 8 9 BSF 12 11 10 09 08 07 06 05

Table of Contents

Golden Queen 2

Bunny and Bunco 9

Red Lady 16

Duke and Queenie 23

Teddy 29

Werty 39

Werty's Money 44

Tatters 50

Gus, Brownie, and Fig 57

Golden Queen

Anna lived on a farm. There were no children to play with. But Anna had a big dog called Golden Queen.

Anna and Golden Queen liked being on a farm. They played together every day. They walked over the fields and in the woods. Once when Anna was lost in a cornfield and the sun went down, Golden Queen found the way out.

Everyone has to learn to work on a big farm. Anna helped her mother and father with the work. She learned to help with the corn. She learned to look after the chickens and the sheep and the cows. She learned always to shut the gate to the pasture where Tony, the big black bull, lived. Tony was very big. He had big horns, and you could never tell what he would do.

Golden Queen learned to work on the farm too. She followed Anna.

Golden Queen learned not to walk on the little corn when it first came up. She learned to keep the cats away from the little chickens.

Golden Queen could tell which sheep was the leader. All the sheep would follow the leader.

Golden Queen could take the leader and all the other sheep from the barn to the pasture, and not one sheep would be lost.

Every day Golden Queen would help Anna bring in the cows from the pasture to the milking barn where Father milked them. Some of the cows would be far away in the pasture when it was time for them to be milked.

Golden Queen would run after the cows. She would bark at them. Then the cows would go to the milking barn.

But Golden Queen would not have anything to do with Tony, the big black bull with the horns.

When Tony saw Golden Queen in his pasture, he would put his head down and run after the big dog. Golden Queen would run as fast as she could because Tony could hurt a dog or a person with his big horns.

One day after Anna had put the cows in the milking barn, she saw that the gate to Tony's pasture was open. She went to shut it because her mother had said that the gate to the pasture where Tony lived must always be shut. Anna saw that she had to go into the pasture to pull the gate shut.

Tony, the big black bull, saw Anna. He did not want Anna in his pasture.

Tony put his head down. He ran at Anna. Golden Queen saw that Tony would hurt Anna with his big horns.

Anna was afraid. She heard Tony coming at her. She jumped away, but she fell as she did so. Tony was running right at Anna. Golden Queen saw that she must stop Tony. So she jumped at Tony's legs and bit them again and again.

Tony had to stop. His legs hurt very much. He wanted to stop that dog that was hurting his legs. So he tried to get at Golden Queen.

The dog bit the bull again and again. Then Golden Queen jumped away before Tony could get her. The big bull could not get at Golden Queen with his horns. The big bull gave up and ran away as fast as he could go.

Golden Queen ran back to Anna to see whether she was all right. Father, who had been in the milking barn, came running. He had a big stick, but he did not have to use it. He took Anna into the house to see whether she was all right because Anna had hurt her leg when she fell. Golden Queen walked right into the house too.

Anna told Mother and Father what Golden Queen had done. Father and Mother both said that if it had not been for Golden Queen, Tony would have hurt Anna more.

Golden Queen lived to be a very old dog. When Mother and Father looked at her, they always wanted to thank her for what she had done when Tony, the big black bull, had tried to hurt Anna.

Bunny and Bunco

Bunny was a little girl. And Bunco was her dog. Every day you could see Bunny and Bunco out walking. Sometimes they would be going to the store to get some bread. Sometimes they would just be taking a walk together.

Bunco always took very good care of Bunny. He watched for cars when they came to streets. Bunny must not get hurt.

Bunny got Bunco as a puppy when Mother went away to take care of Grandfather, who was ill.

"The puppy's name is 'Bunco,'" said Mother. "Take good care of this puppy, and he will take care of you."

Daddy was happy to have Bunco, too, because it was very lonesome without Mother.

Bunco grew to be a big brown dog. He came to know that he was to look after Daddy and Bunny.

At first Bunco barked and barked at the mail carrier. But he had learned that Daddy was very happy to see the mail carrier. Daddy would laugh when the mail carrier had a letter from Mother.

Then Bunco barked and barked at the newspaper carrier. But Bunco soon learned that the newspaper carrier came every day with a newspaper.

But there was one person who did not come every day. Daddy told Bunco that this person was all right. This person would come right into the house. This person would look at the gas meter and write something in a book that she carried.

Bunco did not know what to make of the gas meter reader. Bunco barked and barked and barked at the gas meter reader.

The gas meter reader only laughed and said, "You are a good watchdog."

"Bunco is the best watchdog that ever lived," said Bunny. "He looks after Daddy, and he looks after me now that Mother is away."

As Bunco grew he learned not to bark at friends.

When someone came to the house, Daddy would say, "Bunco, this is one of my friends." And Bunco would know he was not to bark.

He never barked at the children Bunny played with. They all loved Bunco, and they had many good times playing together.

But one night Bunco was asleep in the little room where Daddy let him have his bed. Daddy and Bunny were asleep in their bedrooms. In his sleep Bunco heard a noise. Bunco woke up. He heard someone coming up the walk to the door.

Bunco went to the door and gave a little bark. He knew someone was by the door. But that someone was very quiet.

Then Bunco heard someone walking in the grass around the house. Then he heard someone at the back door. Bunco ran to the back door. Someone tried to open the back door. Bunco jumped at the door and barked.

This was no friend. Friends came in the daytime. This was someone who was trying to get into the house at night.

Bunco was not going to let anyone get into the house and hurt Daddy and Bunny.

Then Bunco heard a noise at the window. Someone was trying to open the window!

Bunco ran and jumped up at the window. He could see a woman. And this woman was no friend.

The woman went away from the window. Bunco heard her walking around the house. Then Bunco heard the doorbell ring. Bunco ran to the door and barked and barked.

Pretty soon Daddy came out of the bedroom looking very much like he had been asleep. And Bunny came out of her room too.

"Bunco, Bunco," said Daddy, "who is at the door at this time of night?"

Bunco barked and barked. He tried to tell Daddy that a woman wanted to get into the house.

Daddy looked out the window. Then he opened the door. Bunco tried to jump at the woman. But Daddy put his arms around the woman and started to laugh and cry all at once. Bunny jumped up and down and cried, "Mother, Mother, Mother."

Bunco had not seen Mother for more than a year. But he saw that this woman must be a friend because Bunny and Daddy were so happy to see her.

"You have a good watchdog," said Mother. "I could not get into my own house."

"You should not come in the night without telling us," said Daddy.

"I got a ride on an airplane, and I did not have time to let you know," said Mother. "I wanted to surprise you."

"You did surprise us. You surprised us very much. But you did not think about Bunco," said Bunny. "Bunco looked after Daddy and me when you were away."

Everyone was so happy. Now Bunco did not want to bark at all. He just sat and watched his family.

Red Lady

Mrs. Curtis did not like dogs. So when Mr. Curtis came home with Red Lady, Mrs. Curtis was not very happy about it.

"Little Harry is growing up, and he should have a dog," said Mr. Curtis.

"Little Harry is only three," said Mrs. Curtis. "What would he want with a big dog?"

"Red Lady and Little Harry can grow up together," said Mr. Curtis. "They will be friends. I think children should have a dog for a friend."

"Well," said Mrs. Curtis, "you will have to make a doghouse. Red Lady will have to live in the backyard. I cannot have a big dog in the house."

In the day, Red Lady played with Little Harry on the grass in the backyard. They played ball. But never once did Red Lady try to bite Little Harry. And when Little Harry went to sleep in the grass, Red Lady lay at his feet. But at night when Mrs. Curtis put Little Harry to bed, Red Lady went to sleep in the doghouse in the backyard.

One day Mr. Curtis came home very happy.

"In three days we can go on our vacation," he said.

"Good," said Mrs. Curtis. "Are we going to the lake again?"

"Yes," said Mr. Curtis. "I have taken a house right by the lake."

"Who will look after Red Lady for us when we are away?" asked Mrs. Curtis.

"We shall take Red Lady with us," said Mr. Curtis.

"I don't think I will like to have Red Lady on our vacation," said Mrs. Curtis.

"Red Lady will play with Little Harry. She will help look after him," said Mr. Curtis.

The day came for Mr. and Mrs. Curtis and Little Harry to drive to the lake. Red Lady watched everything. She knew Little Harry was going away. Red Lady was very unhappy. She went out in the backyard and went into the doghouse. Then she heard Mr. Curtis calling, "Red Lady, Red Lady, come here."

Red Lady ran around the house with her head up.

Mr. Curtis opened the door to the car. "Get in, Red Lady," he said. "You are going on a vacation too."

Red Lady was a very happy dog. She and Little Harry sat together in the car. Pretty soon Red Lady went to sleep. It was a long ride to the lake. And Little Harry went to sleep, too, with his hand on Red Lady.

Little Harry and Red Lady had fun together at the lake. They played in the woods. They played in the water. And always Red Lady watched Little Harry so he would not get hurt.

Right by the house at the lake was a dock that went out into the water. Mr. Curtis got into the boat at the dock and went fishing. Mrs. Curtis sat in a chair to watch Mr. Curtis out on the lake.

Little Harry and Red Lady were playing together. They were playing a game of Try to Find Me. Little Harry would go behind a tree, and then Red Lady would run and find him. The little boy and the big red dog thought Try to Find Me was a good game.

Mrs. Curtis saw Little Harry and Red Lady playing their game. She then went into the house to get something.

Little Harry got tired of playing Try to Find Me. He wanted to play on the dock. He ran down to the water and out onto the dock. Red Lady ran right after him because she knew that Little Harry must not run out onto the dock.

Red Lady barked and barked. Little Harry ran right on. Then he fell on the dock and went right into the water.

Little Harry could not swim! At once Red Lady jumped into the water. She took hold of Little Harry to keep his head out of the water. Then she started to swim.

Mrs. Curtis heard Red Lady barking. She came out of the house. Mrs. Curtis looked around, and she did not see Little Harry or Red Lady. Then Mrs. Curtis ran to the dock as fast as she could run.

Mrs. Curtis saw Red Lady swim with Little Harry. The dog was bringing the little boy out of the water.

Mr. Curtis had come back from fishing when he saw Little Harry fall off the dock. He helped Red Lady get Little Harry out of the water. Mr. Curtis took the little wet boy in his arms.

Mrs. Curtis was laughing and crying all at once. She had the big wet dog in her arms, and she was as wet as Little Harry. Red Lady was trying to tell her that everything was all right.

"I am so happy that Red Lady came with us on our vacation," said Mrs. Curtis.

From that time on, Red Lady never went to sleep in a doghouse again. She always went to sleep right by Little Harry's bed. And Red Lady was very happy.

Duke and Queenie

Duke was a very big dog. He lived with Mrs. and Mr. Byron in a beautiful house on a farm.

Duke tried to look after everything at the beautiful house. He tried to look after everything on the farm too. He would walk around looking to see that all the chickens were in the chicken yard and that all the horses were in the field.

Duke would watch anyone who came to the house to see whether they were friends. Because he was a very big dog, one bark would make anyone who was not a friend go away.

One day Mrs. Byron went to see a friend, and when she came back, she had with her a little dog named Queenie. How Mr. Byron laughed when he saw Queenie, because Queenie was only as big as Mr. Byron's two hands.

Queenie was a happy little dog. She ran around the house and put her nose into everything. Everyone loved Queenie. That is, everyone but Duke.

At first Duke would not look at Queenie. Queenie would bark her little bark and play around Duke's big paws. She would sometimes try to bite him. But Duke would not look at Queenie.

Then Queenie would bark and bark. But she could not get Duke to look at her. Duke would get tired of all the noise at his feet. Then he would bark. Queenie would run away.

Mrs. Byron was afraid Duke would hurt Queenie.

Mr. Byron knew Duke would not hurt anything that was in the house or the yard. But Mr. Byron would say to Mrs. Byron, "Yes, you are going to have to watch Queenie. One of these days Duke will open his mouth, take a big bite, and there will be no Queenie."

Then one day Mr. and Mrs. Byron wanted to take a vacation. They were going to be away a long time. Some friends were coming to live in their beautiful house.

These friends said they could take care of Queenie. But they were afraid of Duke because he was a very big dog. So Mr. Byron took Duke to some friends of his, Mr. and Mrs. Adams, who lived down the road.

Duke was very unhappy in his new home. Mr. Adams fenced Duke so he would not run away. All day Duke lay with his head on his paws.

When Mrs. Adams gave Duke a dish of dog food, Duke would not eat. Mrs. Adams tried to get him to play with a stick. But Duke just lay by the fence with his head on his paws and would not play.

One day when Mr. and Mrs. Adams were in the house, Duke jumped the fence and ran away.

Mr. and Mrs. Adams could not find Duke. They got into their car and went to Mr. Byron's house.

Queenie was happy to see them. She jumped all about and barked and barked her little bark. But no one had seen Duke.

Mr. and Mrs. Adams did not know what to do. They had told Mr. Byron they would take good care of Duke.

Mr. and Mrs. Adams went back to Mr. Byron's house again to see whether Duke had come back. But this time there was no Queenie to bark at them. And no one had seen Duke. Everyone said Queenie and Duke had both run away.

Two days went by. Then as Mrs. Adams went out to get the mail from the mailbox, she saw a very big dog coming down the road. It was Duke. He was carrying Queenie in his mouth just like a mother cat carries her kitten.

Duke put Queenie down at Mrs. Adams's feet. Then he showed in every way he could that he wanted Queenie to be with him. He showed Queenie his water dish and his bed. He ran to Mrs. Adams again and looked up at her as if to say, "Please give us something to eat."

Mrs. Adams liked dogs, and she could tell what Duke wanted to say. She gave the dogs a dish of food. She found a small box for Queenie to sleep in. And Duke was happy.

Then Mrs. Adams wrote a letter to Mrs. Byron and told her about Duke and Queenie. She said she would keep both dogs at her house because Duke would not eat if Queenie was not with him.

From that time on Duke and Queenie were always together. They played together, and they went to sleep together. It was a funny thing to see a very big dog trying to play with a very little dog.

Queenie learned to ride on Duke's back. But when Duke wanted to get Queenie somewhere, he would take her in his mouth and carry her like a mother cat carries a kitten. And never once did Duke hurt Queenie in any way.

Teddy

When Teddy went to his new home, all
the children were fast asleep. The children
were not little boys and girls. They were
big boys and girls who went to school. But
they all loved dogs.

It was nighttime, but Mother got them all up because she knew they would want to see the new puppy.

Teddy was very little. He was like a round ball, and he had beautiful red hair. He had big brown eyes. When Teddy started to play, the brown eyes were full of fun.

The children loved Teddy right away. They said he was a very beautiful little puppy.

Teddy knew he would like this new home. Teddy loved all the children. That first night he went to sleep in John's arms.

All the family was afraid Teddy would get lost. Father went to the store and got Teddy a little collar and a long leash.

Marguerite and Eleanor put the collar on Teddy. They put the leash on the collar. Then they took Teddy for a walk.

Teddy had a good time on his first walk in the city.

But Teddy had to learn many new things on his first walk in the city. Teddy had to learn that little puppies must not go into the street.

In the city the street is full of cars that could hurt little puppies. Teddy had to learn he must follow just the one who was taking him for a walk.

Teddy did his best to please. But one thing Teddy did not learn that first day was to come when his name was called.

When he lived with his mother in the barn on the farm, no one had ever called him "Teddy." He did not know that "Teddy" was the new name John had given him.

When Teddy got home from his first walk, he was a very tired little puppy. He went to sleep in his new bed that the children had made out of a box.

After a long time Teddy woke up. He cried a little because at first he did not know where he was. No one came to him, and so he cried again. But no one came.

Then Teddy cried and cried. He heard a door open. Edward said, "Are you a lonesome little puppy because the family is not at home?"

Teddy jumped and jumped. He barked his baby bark. He was so happy to see Edward.

Edward sat on the floor and played with Teddy. Then he said, "Little puppy, I think you want some food."

Edward got some food and put it into a dish. He put a paper on the floor. And he put the dish of food on the paper. Teddy liked the food very much.

"And now, Teddy," said Edward, "I will take you for a walk. I will take you to the park where you can run around on the green grass."

Edward got the leash and put it onto Teddy's collar. He started up the street with the little puppy following him.

They walked and they walked. Pretty soon they came to a park. There were trees and beautiful green grass all around.

Teddy was very happy. This was just like his old home on the farm. He wanted to run and run and run. But he could not run far. The leash made him fall over on his little nose. And so Edward took the leash from Teddy's collar.

Teddy was just as happy as a little puppy could be. He ran and ran with his nose down, smelling the good smells in the grass. Before long Teddy was over the hill. Edward could not see him.

Edward called, "Teddy, Teddy, come here, Teddy, Teddy!"

But Teddy did not know his name. He just ran on and on and smelled the good smells in the grass.

But the sun was going down, and it was getting dark. Teddy did not come when he was called. Edward could not see the red puppy.

Soon it was dark in the park. Edward called and called, "Teddy!"

Edward knew he must find the puppy. Who would help him find Teddy?

Edward went to the police station and told the police how he had lost a very little puppy with red hair in the park. Would the police please help him find the little puppy?

Edward told the police just what Teddy looked like and just how big he was. The police said that all the police cars would look out for a very little puppy with red hair.

Then Edward went to the radio station. He told the man there that a little red puppy had been lost in the park.

The man at the radio station told everyone over the radio to look out for a little red puppy that was lost.

That was all Edward could think of to do to find the lost puppy. It was very dark, and he must go home and tell the family about Teddy.

The family was afraid they would never see their little red puppy again.

Father called the police station. But no one had heard that a lost red puppy had been found.

Mother called the radio station. But no one had told the radio station that a lost red puppy had been found.

The family went to bed. And some of them cried a little before they went to sleep.

Now what did the little red puppy do in the park?

The little red puppy ran and ran and smelled and smelled. He got very tired. And so he just went to sleep under a tree. When he woke up, it was very dark.

Teddy cried a little because he was lonesome. It was very dark, and he could not see anything. But he could smell. Teddy could smell where he had run around in the grass.

Pretty soon he smelled a new smell. He could smell where Edward had been walking.

Edward had given Teddy some food. Teddy wanted some more food. He wanted to find Edward. Smelling every bit of the way, Teddy followed Edward.

It took a long, long time for the little puppy to smell his way back to his new home. But after a long time, he got to the house. It was the right house because his nose told him that Edward had been at the door.

Teddy barked his baby bark and cried and cried. He cried and cried again and again.

Edward had not been sleeping very well. He woke up, and he heard a puppy crying. Then he heard a puppy crying again and again.

Edward jumped out of bed and ran to the door. When he opened the door, there was a tired, little red puppy.

Teddy looked up at Edward as if to say, "Where have you been? Why did it take you so long to come and open this door and let me in?"

Teddy lived to be an old, old dog. He loved his family very much.

Werty

Werty is a very funny name for a dog. And I don't think there has ever before been a dog named Werty. This is how Werty got her name.

It was a cold day. There was much snow on the streets of the town. An unhappy-looking dog came into the office of the newspaper. She was a friendly dog, and the people in the office liked her. They gave her something to eat and let her sleep in the office.

The snow fell and fell, and it was very cold. The people could not put the dog out in the cold. They made her a warm bed in a big box. The dog made friends with everyone. She did not get in anyone's way.

The people liked the dog and let her stay on in the office of the newspaper. And the dog liked her new home very much.

But the people did not know what to name their new dog. She was a newspaper dog, and they wanted a newspaper name for her.

Then one of the people wrote some letters from a computer that the newspaper people used. This is how the letters looked—QWERTYUIOP.

"Let us take five of these letters from the computer," said the people, "and give our dog a newspaper name."

That is how the newspaper dog got the name Werty.

One day the people in the newspaper office found a little puppy in Werty's bed. The people all said Werty had a beautiful baby.

The day after that, the people found not one little puppy but eight little puppies in Werty's bed. They did not know what to do with so many puppies. They started to think of names for them.

Now the head woman in the office did not like dogs very much. She thought the people in the newspaper office were all taking too much time to care for one big dog and eight little puppies.

So the head woman said they could not keep the dog any longer. The mother and her puppies had to go.

The other people did not know what to do. They loved the dogs very much. They wanted the dogs to have a good home. So one of them wrote about Werty and her puppies on a computer and put it into the paper.

When the people in the town read the newspaper, they wanted to see the dogs. So many people came to the newspaper office to see the puppies that the office was full of people all day long.

A picture of Werty and her eight little puppies was put in the newspaper. And every day one of the people in the newspaper office wrote something about Werty and her family. The people in the town read about Werty every day.

The woman who was head of the office knew that many people were reading her paper. She showed the puppies to everyone. She did not say that the mother and her puppies had to go.

Werty's Money

Werty and the people in the newspaper office took good care of the puppies. The puppies grew and grew. They ran around the office and got in everyone's way.

The puppies barked when people came into the office. Eight puppies can make a lot of noise.

Werty and her puppies ate a lot of food too. Every day the people at the office put money into a box. Then one of the people would go to the store and buy food for the dogs. It took a lot of money every day to buy food for Werty and her eight puppies.

Then the woman who was head of the office, who did not like dogs, said, "A newspaper office is no place to bring up a family of dogs. They eat too much, and they make too much noise. The dogs cannot stay."

The people at the newspaper office made a place for the puppies in the backyard.

All the boys and girls in town came to see the puppies. But the puppies barked and made a lot of noise.

One of the people put a box at the door of the newspaper office. Just over the box she wrote:

WERTY AND HER PUPPIES MUST HAVE FOOD. PUT FOOD MONEY INTO THIS BOX.

At once the people put money into the box for Werty and her puppies. The children put in their money. The people at the newspaper office put in some money.

Every day there was a lot of money in the box. There was much more money than the people had to have to buy food.

What should be done with all the money?

The people at the office said that Werty should have money in the bank. So they took the money to the bank and put it under Werty's name. More and more money was put into the bank every day.

The woman who was head of the newspaper office did not say anything because everyone in town wanted to know about the newspaper dog who had money in the bank.

Then one of the people at the newspaper office wrote something and put it into the paper. It said:

PLEASE HELP ME

Werty is my name. I am a mother dog with four little boys and four little girls. I cannot think of names for my puppies. Please help me. Send to this newspaper four boys' names and four girls' names for my puppies. And send your name too. If I give one of my puppies the name you send to me, I will send you ten dollars.

Many, many boys' names and many, many girls' names came to the newspaper office.

The people in the newspaper office had to find the best names. And when the puppies had all been given their names, Werty gave ten dollars from the bank to each person who thought of one of the names.

There was more and more money in the bank for Werty. The people at the newspaper office got pretty new collars for the puppies, who were getting big. Each puppy had its own collar with its name on it. Then the people in the newspaper office took a picture of Werty and her family.

The picture was put in the newspaper, and under the picture it said:

WHO WILL GIVE ONE OF MY PUPPIES A GOOD HOME?

There were many people who wanted one of Werty's puppies. After a time, each puppy had a new home. Only Werty was now at the newspaper office.

By this time, many people knew about the newspaper office that had a dog with the newspaper name of Werty. They knew about Werty's eight puppies and her many dollars in the bank. The head of the newspaper office, who did not like dogs, said that the newspaper office must keep Werty.

Tatters

Once a boy named Ethan was going to have a birthday. He was going to be five years old. The one thing Ethan wanted was a dog. He did not want any new toys. He wanted a dog to play with.

Mother and Father thought about getting Ethan a dog.

"We cannot buy a dog," said Mother. "We do not have the money."

"If a dog has no home," said Father, "he is taken to the dog pound. Sometimes there is a dog at the dog pound that would like a good home and that would be a good friend for a little boy."

So Father and Mother and Ethan went to the dog pound. And as soon as Ethan saw Tatters, he fell in love with him.

Tatters was not a very pretty dog. He did not have much of a tail. He was black and white and not very clean. But his big brown eyes were just asking for someone to love him. And Ethan loved him as soon as he saw him.

The years went by, and Ethan grew. Soon he was ten years old. And Ethan had a little sister, Carrie, who was three years old. Ethan played with his sister, but he liked to play with Tatters best of all.

Tatters had been the best kind of a family dog. He had looked after Ethan when he started school. When Carrie came, Tatters loved her very much. He looked after Ethan's sister and watched that she was not hurt.

One day Father came home and said, "We are going on a vacation. We are going to drive out and see some places we have never seen before."

What a good time the family had! Mother got their coats and other things. Father and Ethan put good things to eat into a basket. And little Carrie and Tatters ran around the house getting in everyone's way.

Tatters did not know what it was all about, but he could tell that the family was very happy.

"We are going to go on a long ride in the car," said Ethan to Tatters. "And you are going with us."

Tatters was very happy when he was in the car with Ethan and Carrie. Father and Mother got into the car too. Then the family were off on their vacation.

After a time they came to a beautiful lake by the road.

"Let us stop here and have something to eat," said Mother. "Then we can go on and find a place to sleep for the night."

Mother pulled the car off the road. She took out the basket. Father put out the food. And Ethan and Carrie and Tatters did not know if they had ever had so much fun.

After they had eaten, Mother said she thought she would go to sleep under a tree. Father and Ethan put the things back into the basket. And Carrie and Tatters went off to see what they could find.

Everything was quiet for a time. Then Tatters started to bark. He barked, and he barked, and he barked.

"Please keep that dog quiet," said Mother. "I want to go to sleep. I got tired from the long drive."

But Tatters would not stop barking.

"Tatters is only playing with Carrie," said Father.

"Tatters is playing in a funny way with Carrie," said Ethan. "He is running around and around. And then he jumps at Carrie and pushes her down."

Mother knew that Tatters was trying to take care of Carrie by pushing her down. Mother jumped to her feet and ran to where Carrie was. Tatters was barking at something in the grass. It was a rattlesnake.

Every time Carrie started to go to the rattlesnake, Tatters would push her down. And then he went around and around the rattlesnake, barking as much as he could so the rattlesnake would watch him and not bite Carrie.

Just as Mother got to Carrie, the big rattlesnake bit Tatters. When Tatters saw that Carrie would not get hurt, he went to Mother as fast as his hurt leg would let him.

Father knew that a rattlesnake bite would make Tatters very ill if they did not get him to a doctor right away.

Mother said, "We must find a doctor for Tatters."

So Mother put Tatters and the family into the car. She went as fast as she could to town and found a doctor.

For days Tatters was so ill that he had to stay with the doctor. But then Tatters got well. He is looking after Carrie and Ethan again. And Tatters, the dog that came from the dog pound, is a very happy dog because his family loves him very much.

Gus, Brownie, and Fig

Shelby lived in a warm little house with her mother and father. Their two dogs, Brownie and Fig, and their new puppy, Gus, lived in the house too. The house was on a big farm by a lake.

Every night after supper, Brownie and Fig would go out and run in back of the house, and Father would clean up the supper table. Mother and Shelby would read, and Gus, who was very little, would play on the floor with his toys.

The warm little house was a good place to be after supper. Father would talk and sing as he cleaned the table. And Mother would look up from the book she was reading and laugh. Shelby would sing and talk too.

Every night when Brownie and Fig ran out to play, they went through a little door that was in the big back door. Only Brownie and Fig could go through the little dog door—or so Mother and Father thought.

Mother and Father did not know this, but Gus always watched the dogs go out their little door. It was as if the little puppy thought, "Where do they go?"

One night Brownie and Fig ran out the little door as always. Mother, Father, and Shelby were talking and reading as always. But on this night, Gus did not want to play with his toys. He wanted to see where Brownie and Fig went. So he jumped up and went through the little dog door. Then Gus ran out into the dark night.

Mother and Father were talking, and Shelby had her eyes on her book. They did not hear Gus go. Gus was far away before anyone saw that he was not there. At last Shelby looked up from her book and asked, "Where is Gus?"

Mother ran through the house and called, "Gus!" Father opened the big back door and called, "Gus!" Shelby was afraid. They could not find the little puppy.

Gus did not hear Mother. Gus did not hear Father. He was looking for Brownie and Fig. He ran fast on his little legs, and soon he was by the barn. Then he ran down the hill by the lake.

Mother, Father, and Shelby ran out the door and called, "Gus!" But Gus was too far away to hear. He ran, looking for Brownie and Fig. As he ran, Gus fell into a cold puddle by the lake. When he fell, he hurt his leg. The puddle was very, very cold. Gus could not get out of the big puddle. He cried and he cried.

Mother, Father, and Shelby had run the other way and did not hear Gus. But Brownie and Fig did. The dogs were by the barn. When they heard Gus, they ran down the hill. Gus saw them, and he cried and barked some more.

Brownie and Fig knew what to do. Fig ran to the house and barked. Brownie pulled Gus out of the puddle. Then Brownie tried to make the little puppy warm again.

Fig ran and found Mother, Father, and Shelby. He barked until they followed him to Gus and Brownie. Mother picked up Gus and said, "Gus, we found you!"

Father looked at Brownie and Fig and said, "Good dogs!"

When they were all back in the house, Father made a better dog door so that Gus could not run away and get lost again. Mother sat with Gus and said over and over that Brownie and Fig were heroes. Father said they were heroes too.

Shelby was very happy to have her little puppy back. She played with Gus before they went to bed. And Brownie and Fig, the heroes of the day, stayed in the warm house and barked and barked.